THE OFFICIAL
LEEDS
UNITED
ANNUAL 2017

Written by Ryan Parrish

Designed by Mathew Whittles

A Grange Publication

© 2016. Published by Grange Communications Ltd., Edinburgh, under licence from Leeds United Football Club. Printed in the EU.

Photographs © Varley Picture Agency / Yorkshire Evening Post

ISBN 978-1-911287-07-0

WELCOME TO THE OFFICIAL LEEDS UNITED ANNUAL 2017!

As the start of another year draws in, we hope with everything crossed that the next 12 months include a return to the Promised Land for our beloved club.

2015/16 had its fleeting moments of joy and inspiration, but ultimately fell short of expectations and the challenge remains the same this time around.

In this Annual, we will be taking a closer look at those tasked with bringing Premier League football back to Elland Road for the first time in 13 years.

We also welcome Garry Monk to Leeds and get to know the boss who has vowed to bring entertaining football to LS11, profiling his impressive career to date within these pages.

Once you've delved deeper into the world of Leeds United, we have a number of quizzes and puzzles to put your knowledge to the test on all things white, yellow and blue. We hope you enjoy it.

Marching on Together!

CONTENTS

LEEDS UNITED HONOURS

FOOTBALL LEAGUE

1968-69 First Division champions
1973-74 First Division champions
1991-92 First Division champions
1923-24 Second Division champions
1963-64 Second Division champions
1989-90 Second Division champions
1927-28 Second Division runners-up
1931-32 Second Division runners-up
1955-56 Second Division runners-up
2009-10 League One runners-up

FA CUP

1972 FA Cup winners
1965 FA Cup finalists
1970 FA Cup finalists
1973 FA Cup finalists

FOOTBALL LEAGUE CUP

1968 Football League Cup winners
1996 Football League Cup finalists

CHARITY SHIELD

1969 FA Charity Shield winners
1992 FA Charity Shield winners
1974 FA Charity Shield runners-up

FA YOUTH CUP

1993 FA Youth Cup winners
1997 FA Youth Cup winners

EUROPEAN CUP

1974-75 European Cup finalists

EUROPEAN CUP WINNERS' CUP

1972-73 European Cup Winners' Cup finalists

INTER CITIES FAIRS CUP/UEFA CUP

1967-68 European Fairs Cup winners
1970-71 European Fairs Cup winners
1966-67 European Fairs Cup finalists

HIGHLIGHTS OF 2015/16

2015/16 proved to be another season of ups and downs for the Whites. Month by month, we take a look back at the last campaign and pick out some of the highlights along the way…

AUGUST

Results

Leeds United 1 (Antenucci 83)
Burnley 1 (Vokes 86)

Doncaster Rovers 1 (Williams pen 31)
Leeds United 1 (Cook 14)
League Cup (lost 2-4 on penalties)

Reading 0, Leeds United 0

Bristol City 2 (Agard 89, Flint 90+5)
Leeds United 2 (Antenucci pen 39, Wood 52)

Leeds United 1 (Wood 61)
Sheffield Wednesday 1 (Matias 37)

Derby County 1 (Martin 48)
Leeds United 2 (Adeyemi 43, Wood 88)

In ▶ Charlie Horton (Cardiff City), Lee Erwin (Motherwell), Sol Bamba (Palermo), Chris Wood (Leicester City), Tom Adeyemi (Cardiff City, loan), Ross Turnbull (Barnsley), Stuart Dallas (Brentford)

◀ Out Billy Sharp (Sheffield United), Steve Morison (Millwall), Nick Ajose (Swindon Town)

Highlights

vs Burnley (1-1 draw)
Saturday August 8, 2015
Elland Road

Following a summer which included the appointment of head coach Uwe Rosler and the signings of Chris Wood, Stuart Dallas and Sol Bamba among others, United's 2015/16 campaign got underway with an enthralling 1-1 draw at home to newly-relegated Burnley. Mirco Antenucci opened the scoring to raise the roof at Elland Road after 83 minutes, netting a sensational curling effort which looked to put the hosts on course for a winning start, only for former United loanee Sam Vokes to head home an equaliser three minutes later.

vs Derby County (2-1 win)
Saturday August 29, 2015
iPro Stadium

Despite exiting the Capital One Cup on penalties at Doncaster Rovers five days on from the opening day draw with Burnley, United remained unbeaten in the league during the early weeks of the season but were made to wait until the final weekend of August to secure their first three points. They came in dramatic fashion too, with Chris Wood thundering an 88th-minute winner in off the post after promotion hopefuls Derby had pulled themselves level to cancel out a towering header from on-loan midfielder Tom Adeyemi.

SEPTEMBER

Results

Leeds United 1 (Antenucci 76)
Brentford 1 (Djuricin 29)

Leeds United 0
Ipswich Town 1 (Smith 32)

MK Dons 1 (Church 74)
Leeds United 2 (Wood pen 31, Taylor 43)

Middlesbrough 3 (Nugent 3, Bellusci OG 32, Fabbrini 81)
Leeds United 0

In ▶ Jordan Botaka (Excelsior)

Highlights

vs MK Dons (2-1 win)
Saturday September 19, 2015
Stadium mk

United returned from the season's first international break to record a 1-1 draw with Brentford before slipping to a first Championship defeat of the campaign at home to Ipswich Town. Amends were made the following weekend, though, as a Charlie Taylor-inspired performance secured the three points in front of 6,297 travelling fans. Taylor's lung-busting run drew the penalty for Wood to open the scoring at Stadium mk, before the full-back netted his first senior goal for the club with a precise strike into the bottom corner.

7

OCTOBER

Results

Leeds United 0,
Birmingham City 2 (Gray 31, Maghoma 90+1)

Leeds United 1 (Cooper 22)
Brighton & Hove Albion 2 (March 14, Zamora 89)

Fulham 1 (Dembele 23)
Leeds United 1 (Wood pen 64)

Bolton Wanderers 1 (Ameobi 32)
Leeds United 1 (Antenucci pen 71)

Leeds United 0,
Blackburn Rovers 2 (Conway 1, Rhodes 6)

In ▶ Will Buckley (Sunderland, loan)

◀ Out Lee Erwin (Bury, loan)

NOVEMBER

Results

Leeds United 1 (Mowatt 63)
Cardiff City 0

Huddersfield Town 0
Leeds United 3 (Antenucci 45+5, Wood 45+7, Mowatt 54)

Leeds United 0
Rotherham United 1 (Newell 54)

Queens Park Rangers 1 (Austin 58)
Leeds United 0

In ▶ Liam Bridcutt (Sunderland, loan)

◀ Out Ross Killock (Stockport County, loan), Will
Buckley (Sunderland, loan terminated), Charlie
Horton (mutual consent)

Highlights

vs Cardiff City (1-0 win)
Tuesday November 3, 2015
Elland Road

United endured a winless October and, after 12 games
in charge, Rosler was replaced by former Rotherham
boss Steve Evans, who oversaw draws at Fulham and
Bolton before suffering defeat at home to Blackburn
in his first three matches. His fourth game at the helm
however, a midweek visit of Cardiff City, saw United
end an eight-month wait for victory on home soil
courtesy of a trademark Alex Mowatt thunderbolt.
Mowatt struck just after the hour mark to secure
United's first win over the Bluebirds in 31 years.

vs Huddersfield Town (3-0 win)
Saturday November 7, 2015
John Smith's Stadium

Four days on from the uplifting victory against Cardiff,
United made it back-to-back wins for the first time all
season with an emphatic Yorkshire derby demolition of
Huddersfield Town. After a cagey opening 45 minutes
at the John Smith's Stadium, quick-fire goals from
Antenucci and Wood deep into first-half stoppage
time suddenly gave Evans' side a comfortable lead
going into the break. Mowatt then hit his second
wonder-strike in as many matches shortly after the
restart to wrap up a fourth consecutive win over
United's nearest Championship rivals.

DECEMBER

Results

Leeds United 2 (Wood 30, Adeyemi 45)
Hull City 1 (Elmohamady 51)

Charlton Athletic 0
Leeds United 0

Wolverhampton Wanderers 2 (Afobe 10, Byrne 81)
Leeds United 3 (Byram 44 & 60, Dallas 51)

Leeds United 1 (Browne OG 46)
Preston North End 0

Nottingham Forest 1 (Oliveira 17)
Leeds United 1 (Byram 80)

Leeds United 2 (Bamba 42, Wood 71)
Derby County 2 (Hendrick 13, Ince 78)

Highlights

vs Hull City (2-1 win)
Saturday December 5, 2015
Elland Road

Consecutive defeats to Rotherham and Queens Park Rangers dampened the derby joys of Huddersfield, but United bounced back by embarking on an unbeaten December which saw the team climb the Championship table, starting with an impressive victory at home to high-flying Hull City. Adeyemi and Wood were on target during a dominant first half to take a deserved two-goal cushion into the break, before Ahmed Elmohamady pulled one back in the second half to set up a nervy finale, with United forced to withstand plenty of Hull pressure.

vs Wolverhampton Wanderers (3-2 win)
Thursday December 17, 2015
Molineux Stadium

A goalless draw at Charlton followed the win over Hull, before United headed to Stadium for a televised midweek clash which saw Sam Byram mark his return to the team in spectacular fashion. Byram, who would join Premier League side West Ham the following month, slotted home on the stroke of half-time to cancel out Benik Afobe's opener. Stuart Dallas then rifled in his first goal for the club before Byram netted his second of the evening with a towering header. Wolves pulled one back but Leeds held firm.

JANUARY

Results

Leeds United 1 (Kay OG 87)
MK Dons 1 (Hall 30)

Leeds United 2 (Carayol 45, Doukara 90)
Rotherham United 0
FA Cup Third Round

Ipswich Town 2 (Chambers 50, Pitman 90+2)
Leeds United 1 (Doukara 1)

Sheffield Wednesday 2 (Hooper 47 & 50)
Leeds United 0

Leeds United 1 (Doukara 59)
Bristol City 0

Brentford 1 (Saunders 27)
Leeds United 1 (Carayol 84)

Bolton Wanderers 1 (Pratley 80),
Leeds United 2 (Doukara 9, Diagouraga 39)
FA Cup Fourth Round

In ▶ Mustapha Carayol (Middlesbrough, loan), Toumani Diagouraga (Brentford), Jack McKay (Doncaster Rovers), Paul McKay (Doncaster Rovers)

◀ Out Sam Byram (West Ham United), Robbie McDaid (Lincoln City, loan), Tommaso Bianchi (Ascoli, loan), Chris Dawson (Rotherham United)

Highlights

vs Bolton Wanderers (2-1 win)
FA Cup Fourth Round
Saturday January 30, 2016
Macron Stadium

United made a mixed start to the new year but a 2-0 FA Cup victory at home to Rotherham teed up this Fourth Round trip to the Macron Stadium. In-form Souleymane Doukara netted his fourth goal in six matches to open the scoring after just nine minutes, before full debutant Toumani Diagouraga – signed from Brentford at the start of the week – doubled the advantage with a composed finish shortly before half-time. United's progression was sealed, despite the hosts grabbing a consolation goal late on.

FEBRUARY

Results

Leeds United 0
Nottingham Forest 1 (Oliveira 60)

Leeds United 0
Middlesbrough 0

Watford 1 (Wootton OG 54)
Leeds United 0
FA Cup Fifth Round

Leeds United 1 (Cook 38)
Fulham 1 (Cairney 17)

Brighton & Hove Albion 4 (Hemed pen 18 & 28, Cooper OG 22, Dunk 38)
Leeds United 0

MARCH

‖‖

Results

Leeds United 2 (Antenucci 39 & 62)
Bolton Wanderers 1 (Woolery 74)

Cardiff City 0
Leeds United 2 (Doukara 37, Antenucci 90+4)

Blackburn Rovers 1 (Jackson 89)
Leeds United 2 (Bamba 34, Antenucci 69)

Leeds United 1 (Dallas 22)
Huddersfield Town 4 (Hudson 41, Bunn 69, Matmour 73, Wells 77)

◀ **Out** Luke Parkin (mutual consent)

Highlights

vs Cardiff City (2-0 win)
Tuesday March 8, 2016
Cardiff City Stadium

February passed without victory and United owed a response to the travelling fans who witnessed a humiliating 4-0 defeat at Brighton. Bolton were beaten 2-1 at Elland Road the following Saturday, before Evans' side truly made amends by clinching an unexpected seasonal double over Cardiff in South Wales. Doukara was back among the goals, firing United ahead after 37 minutes, but the three points owed plenty to the heroics of Marco Silvestri, who kept the visitors in it before Antenucci wrapped things up in stoppage time.

APRIL

Results

Rotherham United 2 (Frecklington 27, Halford pen 90)
Leeds United 1 (Murphy 79)

Leeds United 1 (Wood 70)
Queens Park Rangers 1 (Chery pen 87)

Burnley 1 (Arfield 1)
Leeds United 0

Birmingham City 1 (Donaldson 53)
Leeds United 2 (Dallas 11 & 50)

Leeds United 3 (Diagouraga 48, Wood 69 & 85)
Reading 2 (Hector 39, Rakels 81)

Leeds United 2 (Bamba 60, Diagouraga 64)
Wolverhampton Wanderers 1 (Saville 77)

Hull City 2 (Hernandez 45+1, Huddlestone 45+3)
Leeds United 2 (Wood 15, Dallas 88)

Leeds United 1 (Bamba 71)
Charlton Athletic 2 (Gudmundsson 39, Lookman 49)

2015/16 Leeds United top appearance makers:

Stuart Dallas (49)
Marco Silvestri (48)
Lewis Cook (47)
Charlie Taylor (43)
Mirco Antenucci (43)
Liam Cooper (41)

Highlights

vs Birmingham City (2-1 win)
Tuesday April 12, 2016
St Andrew's Stadium

United's rearranged trip to the West Midlands came on the back of a four-game winless run, but their dominant display in a harsh 1-0 defeat at eventual champions Burnley the previous Saturday suggested their fortunes could be about to turn. Dallas was in inspired form to ensure that would be the case at St Andrew's, hitting an impressive brace – including a Goal of the Season contender in the second half – before Birmingham threatened a fightback, with Clayton Donaldson on target for the hosts shortly after United's second.

vs Reading (3-2 win)
Saturday April 16, 2016
Elland Road

The victory over Birmingham set United up for an encouraging end to the campaign, with Evans' side putting another three points on the board when former Leeds boss Brian McDermott brought his Reading team to Elland Road. A five-goal thriller saw the hosts fall behind in the first half before turning the game on its head courtesy of efforts from Diagouraga and Wood. The Royals managed to pull themselves back on level terms, but Wood had the final say with his second goal of the afternoon five minutes from time.

Highlights

vs Preston North End
Saturday May 7, 2016
Deepdale

Having suffered defeat to relegated Charlton in their final home game of the season a week earlier, United's campaign was brought to a close with a 1-1 draw away to Simon Grayson's Preston North End. Wood dispatched a second-half penalty to take his tally to 13 for the season and put the visitors in front, but Preston snatched a point in stoppage-time through substitute Jordan Hugill's close-range finish. A share of the spoils meant United finished 2015/16 in 13th – two places higher than the previous year.

MAY

Results

Preston North End 1 (Hugill 90+2)
Leeds United 1 (Wood pen 78)

◀ **Out** Mirco Antenucci, Scott Wootton, Lewis Walters, Eric Grimes, Ross Killock, Jake Skelton, Robbie McDaid, Tom Lyman (all released)

2015/16 Leeds United top goalscorers:

Chris Wood (13)
Stuart Dallas (5)
Sol Bamba (4)

Mirco Antenucci (9)
Souleymane Doukara (5)

Final 2015/16 Championship table

Pos	Team	P	Home					Away					GD	Pts
			W	D	L	GF	GA	W	D	L	GF	GA		
1	Burnley	46	15	6	2	38	14	11	9	3	34	21	37	93
2	Middlesbrough	46	16	5	2	34	8	10	6	7	29	23	32	89
3	Brighton	46	15	5	3	40	18	9	12	2	32	24	30	89
4	Hull	46	15	7	1	47	12	9	4	10	22	23	34	83
5	Derby	46	12	7	4	37	16	9	8	6	29	27	23	78
6	Sheff Wed	46	13	8	2	42	17	6	9	8	24	28	21	74
7	Ipswich	46	9	8	6	28	24	9	7	7	25	27	2	69
8	Cardiff	46	12	9	2	33	20	5	8	10	23	31	5	68
9	Brentford	46	10	4	9	33	30	9	4	10	39	37	5	65
10	Birmingham	46	9	5	9	27	27	7	10	6	26	22	4	63
11	Preston	46	7	10	6	21	21	8	7	8	24	24	0	62
12	QPR	46	10	9	4	37	25	4	9	10	17	29	0	60
13	Leeds	46	7	8	8	23	28	7	9	7	27	30	-8	59
14	Wolves	46	7	10	6	26	26	7	6	10	27	32	-5	58
15	Blackburn	46	8	8	7	29	23	5	8	10	17	23	0	55
16	Nottm Forest	46	7	8	8	25	26	6	8	9	18	21	-4	55
17	Reading	46	8	9	6	25	20	5	4	14	27	39	-7	52
18	Bristol City	46	7	7	9	34	34	6	6	11	20	37	-17	52
19	Huddersfield	46	7	6	10	33	33	6	6	11	26	37	-11	51
20	Fulham	46	8	5	10	36	36	4	10	9	30	43	-13	51
21	Rotherham	46	8	6	9	31	34	5	4	14	22	37	-18	49
22	Charlton	46	5	8	10	23	35	4	5	14	17	45	-40	40
23	MK Dons	46	7	3	13	21	37	2	9	12	18	32	-30	39
24	Bolton	46	5	11	7	24	26	0	4	19	17	55	-40	30

GOALKEEPERS

ROB GREEN

D.O.B.: 18/01/1980 | **NATIONALITY:** English

The former England international was snapped up by Garry Monk on a one-year deal over the summer, shortly after his release from Championship rivals Queens Park Rangers.

Green, a vastly-experienced 'keeper who arrived at Elland Road with over 600 career appearances to his name, progressed through the ranks at Norwich City and enjoyed a six-year stint at West Ham United before joining QPR in 2012.

Green, 36 at the time of putting pen to paper, immediately became the oldest member of the first-team squad upon signing for Leeds back in July and was handed the number 1 shirt in time for the new campaign.

ROSS TURNBULL

D.O.B.: 04/01/1985 | **NATIONALITY:** English

Signed from Barnsley in summer 2015 to provide competition for United's number 1 shirt, the former Middlesbrough and Chelsea man endured a frustrating debut season at Elland Road.

Turnbull was restricted to just one senior appearance last term – coming in a League Cup tie at Doncaster Rovers – after a broken ankle, sustained in a behind-close-doors friendly at Thorp Arch, saw him sidelined for the majority of the campaign.

Turnbull, who is capped by England at Under-19s level and has a Champions League winner's medal to his name, is under contract at Elland Road until the summer.

MARCO SILVESTRI

D.O.B.: 02/03/1991 | **NATIONALITY:** Italian

The agile shot-stopper, a summer 2014 arrival from Serie A side Chievo, missed just one Championship fixture last season.

Silvestri, who has previously represented Italy at Under-21s level, began his career with homeland side Modena before joining Chievo and enjoying loan spells with Reggiana, Padova and Cagliari – the club previously owned by United chairman Massimo Cellino.

After switching to Elland Road on a four-year deal, Silvestri was shortlisted for United's Player of the Year award during his debut season in English football and continues to earn rave reviews between the sticks.

BAILEY PEACOCK-FARRELL

D.O.B.: 29/10/96 | **NATIONALITY:** English

The youngster found himself unexpectedly thrown into the first-team fold last season following injury to Turnbull and the departure of Charlie Horton, but Peacock-Farrell proved an able deputy to Silvestri when handed his senior debut.

The Darlington-born stopper, who joined United from Middlesbrough's Academy in 2013, stepped in for the suspended Silvestri for the visit of Queens Park Rangers and was beaten only by a late penalty in a 1-1 draw.

One year on from signing his first professional contract with the club, Peacock-Farrell penned a new two-year deal at Elland Road over the summer after reportedly attracting Premier League interest.

DEFENDERS

LIAM COOPER

D.O.B.: 30/08/1991 | **NATIONALITY:** Scottish

United's vice-captain made the switch to Elland Road from Chesterfield in summer 2014 after catching the eye in a pre-season friendly against the Whites.

Cooper, a product of Hull City's Academy, has been a regular fixture at the heart of the United defence since his arrival and earned a call-up to the senior Scotland squad for the first time last season.

The left-sided centre-back previously spent time on loan at Carlisle United and Huddersfield Town while on the books of Hull, before earning a place in the League Two PFA Team of the Year 2013/14 as he helped Chesterfield secure promotion.

PONTUS JANSSON

D.O.B.: 13/02/1991 | **NATIONALITY:** Swedish

The Swedish international joined United on a season-long loan from Italian outfit Torino during the second week of the current campaign.

Jansson, a towering six-foot-five centre-back who was part of Sweden's Euro 2016 squad, began his career with homeland side Malmo FF, where he worked under United assistant boss Pep Clotet and won three league titles.

The defender made the switch to Serie A in 2014 and made 25 appearances in all competitions during his two years in Italy before heading to West Yorkshire.

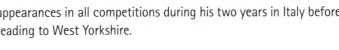

KYLE BARTLEY

D.O.B.: 22/05/1991 | **NATIONALITY:** English

Monk's second signing of the summer saw the United boss reunited with a familiar face as Swansea City centre-back Kyle Bartley arrived on a season-long loan.

Bartley, a former England Under-17s international, played alongside and worked under Monk during his time at the Liberty Stadium after joining from Arsenal in 2012.

The Stockport-born defender, who won the FA Youth Cup and featured in the Champions League during his time with Arsenal, has enjoyed loan spells with Sheffield United, Rangers and Birmingham City in recent years.

GAETANO BERARDI

D.O.B.: 21/08/1988 | **NATIONALITY:** Swiss

The Swiss full-back, signed from Italian outfit Sampdoria in July 2014, is rapidly earning cult hero status at Elland Road for his commitment to the cause in the face of several injury setbacks.

Berardi, who is equally as comfortable playing on the right or the left, endured a testing start to life in English football and was sent off on his United debut, but the defender's solid performances have established him as a key figure in the side and earned him a Player of the Year nomination last season.

Berardi twice won the play-offs during his time in Serie B, with Brescia and Sampdoria.

CHARLIE TAYLOR

D.O.B.: 18/09/1993 | **NATIONALITY:** English

The Thorp Arch graduate capped a fine 2015/16 season by collecting United's Player of the Year award, despite missing a chunk of the campaign through illness.

The York-born full-back, who progressed through the ranks to make his debut as a 17-year-old in 2011, was made to be patient for a regular run in the United side and spent time on loan at Bradford City, York City, Inverness and Fleetwood Town, prior to making the left-back spot his own at the start of 2015.

Taylor, capped by England at Under-19s level, is regarded as one of the brightest prospects in the Championship.

LEWIE COYLE

D.O.B.: 15/10/1995 | **NATIONALITY:** English

The Hull-born full-back has been on United's books since the age of seven and eventually made his first-team debut last season after impressing as captain of the Under-21s.

Coyle, who had a brief loan spell at Harrogate Town in 2014, made his first outing as a late substitute away to Nottingham Forest before being handed a first start at home to Rotherham United in the FA Cup. He went on to end the campaign with 13 appearances to his name.

The Academy product comes from a particularly sporting family, with eldest brother Tommy a professional boxer and second-eldest, Joe, a professional golfer.

LUKE AYLING

D.O.B.: 25/08/1991 | **NATIONALITY:** English

A product of Arsenal's youth system, the versatile defender arrived at Elland Road over the summer following two impressive seasons with Championship rivals Bristol City.

Ayling, who signed a three-year deal with United in August, went straight into Garry Monk's starting line-up and was named Man of the Match following his debut against Birmingham City.

Mainly a right-back throughout his career, Ayling spent four years with Yeovil Town and helped the Glovers achieve promotion from League One before making the switch to Ashton Gate.

MIDFIELDERS

EUNAN O'KANE

D.O.B.: 10/07/1990 | **NATIONALITY:** Irish

The Republic of Ireland international became our 11th and final signing of the summer 2016 transfer window when he arrived on deadline day on a two-year deal from AFC Bournemouth.

O'Kane, who spent time with Everton's Academy as a youngster, made 16 Premier League appearances last season having enjoyed a rise through the divisions in his career so far.

The midfielder joined Bournemouth, then a League One side, from Torquay United in 2012 and helped the Cherries go on to achieve top-flight promotion, making over 100 appearances, during his four-year stay on the South Coast.

LUKE MURPHY

D.O.B.: 21/10/1989 | **NATIONALITY:** English

The summer 2013 signing from Crewe Alexandra is one of United's longest-serving players and entered the new season as the top appearance maker within the current squad.

Murphy, who helped fire Crewe to promotion from League Two in 2012, wasted little time in introducing himself to the Elland Road faithful with a dramatic late winner on his United debut.

The Macclesfield-born midfielder missed the early parts of last season with an injury sustained at the start of the summer and, as a result, he was unable to nail down a regular place in the side for large parts of the campaign.

TOUMANI DIAGOURAGA

D.O.B.: 09/06/1987 | **NATIONALITY:** Malian

After signing from Championship rivals Brentford in January 2016, the former Paris Saint-Germain trainee made his United debut away to the Bees just one day after completing his switch from Griffin Park.

Diagouraga, whose career in English football began at Watford, ended last season with three goals to his name after waiting almost three years since last finding the net. He arrived at Elland Road on a two-and-a-half-year deal not long after being named the Brentford Supporters' Player of the Season.

The Paris-born central-midfielder has been in England for 12 years now and has also had stints at Swindon, Rotherham, Hereford, Peterborough and Portsmouth.

STUART DALLAS

D.O.B.: 19/04/1991 | **NATIONALITY:** Northern Irish

The Northern Ireland international soon settled into life at Elland Road following his summer 2015 move from Brentford, ending his debut campaign as United's Players' Player of the Year after being crowned by his team-mates.

Dallas, who began his career with semi-professional homeland side Crusaders, earning just £70 a week, became the first United player to feature in a major tournament for 10 years when he represented his country at Euro 2016.

The winger, a League One promotion winner with Brentford in 2014, netted five goals last term, including an impressive double away to Birmingham and a late equaliser at Hull.

KALVIN PHILLIPS

D.O.B.: 02/12/1995 | **NATIONALITY:** English

The homegrown central-midfielder scored on his Elland Road debut – a 2-1 defeat to Cardiff City in April 2015 – just five days after making his first senior appearance away to Wolverhampton Wanderers.

Phillips, who joined the club from local side Wortley Juniors in 2010, progressed through the ranks at Thorp Arch and earned a glowing reputation for his all-action displays prior to his first-team breakthrough.

The youngster still featured regularly with the Under-21s last season, though, as he was limited to just 10 Championship appearances in total, with his only three starts coming during the opening month of the campaign.

MATT GRIMES

D.O.B.: 15/07/1995 | **NATIONALITY:** English

The England Under-21s international followed Swansea teammate Bartley in making a season-long loan switch to Elland Road over the summer.

Grimes, originally signed by Monk in early 2015 after catching the eye with hometown club Exeter City, has a handful of Premier League appearances to his name and spent time on loan in the Championship with Blackburn Rovers last season.

The central midfielder, who is seen as a set-piece specialist, joined United with the intention of getting regular first-team football under his belt and adding to his international honours with England's youth teams.

LIAM BRIDCUTT

D.O.B.: 08/05/1989 | **NATIONALITY:** Scottish

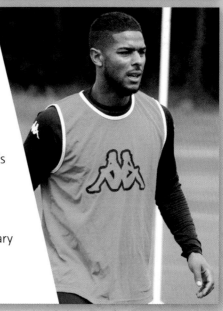

The Scotland international rejoined United permanently last summer on the back of a successful loan spell from Sunderland in 2015/16.

Bridcutt, a product of Chelsea's Academy, was shortlisted for United's Player of the Year award after making a big impression in his 27 appearances in all competitions while on loan at Elland Road.

The central midfielder made his name during a four-year stint with Brighton and earned a Premier League switch to Sunderland in January 2014. Bridcutt penned a two-year deal at Elland Road in August.

PABLO HERNANDEZ

D.O.B.: 11/04/1985 | **NATIONALITY:** Spanish

A Spanish international with over 130 La Liga appearances to his name, the former Swansea City winger became United's seventh summer signing when he joined on loan from Qatari side Al-Arabi.

The experienced Hernandez, who played alongside and worked under Monk during his recent two-year stint at the Liberty Stadium, moved to Elland Road for an initial six-month spell with the option of making his stay permanent.

Hernandez progressed through Valencia's famed youth system and joined Swansea for a then club-record fee in 2012.

ALEX MOWATT

D.O.B.: 13/02/1995 | **NATIONALITY:** English

The Doncaster-born midfielder, another graduate of United's famed Thorp Arch Academy, is renowned for beating Championship goalkeepers from distance with stunning strikes with his deadly left foot.

Mowatt was the club's Player of the Year for 2014/15 and has earned international recognition with England Under-20s, although he often found himself in and out of the United starting line-up last season.

The last campaign saw Mowatt, who first joined his boyhood club aged nine, reach a century of league appearances and score arguably his finest goals in Leeds colours – against Cardiff City and Huddersfield Town – both in the space of four days.

RONALDO VIEIRA

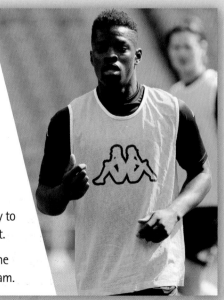

D.O.B.: 20/07/1998 | **NATIONALITY:** Guinea-Bissau (although eligible to play for Portugal)

Born in Guinea-Bissau, but having grown up in Portugal and spent time on the books of European giants Benfica, the highly-rated youngster first arrived at United on trial in 2015 after catching the eye playing for York College.

Vieira, who moved to England with his family in 2011, was thrown into the spotlight during the final week of last season, making his senior debut away to Preston North End just two days after signing his first professional contract.

The central midfielder started 2015/16 as a first-year scholar playing in the Under-18s, but he soon progressed to the Under-21s and into the first team.

KEMAR ROOFE

D.O.B.: 06/01/1993 | **NATIONALITY:** English

Monk bolstered his attacking options by swooping for last season's League Two Player of the Year on a four-year deal from Oxford United back in July.

Roofe, a former West Brom trainee, established himself as one of the Football League's hottest properties during 2015/16 as he helped fire his side to promotion with 26 goals from 49 appearances.

The versatile forward, who played alongside Wood during his time in West Brom's youth system, has previously spent time on loan at Icelandic side Vikingur Reykjavik, as well as homeland clubs Northampton Town, Cheltenham Town and Colchester United.

FORWARDS

HADI SACKO

D.O.B.: 24/03/1994 | **NATIONALITY:** French

Capped by France at Under-20s level, the pacy winger began his career with Bordeaux but was poached by Portuguese giants Sporting Lisbon in 2014.

Sacko, who returned to France last season for a stint with Ligue 2 outfit Sochaux, joined United over the summer on a season-long loan with a view to a permanent deal.

The youngster is yet to feature for Sporting's senior team but has featured over 50 times for their 'B' team. It took Sacko just 13 minutes to score in his first appearance in United colours – a pre-season friendly away to Irish side Shelbourne.

CHRIS WOOD

D.O.B.: 07/12/1991 | **NATIONALITY:** New Zealander

The New Zealand international ended his debut season at Elland Road as United's top goalscorer, finding the net 13 times in 2015/16 following his summer arrival from eventual Premier League champions Leicester City.

Wood, who is the youngest-ever player to captain his country, has achieved promotion with three of his previous clubs – West Brom, Brighton and Leicester. Penning a four-year deal with United saw the centre-forward become the club's most expensive signing outside of the top-flight.

Wood's senior career began with homeland side Cambridge FC, making his debut aged 15, before being brought to England by West Brom back in 2009.

MARCUS ANTONSSON

D.O.B.: 08/05/1991 | **NATIONALITY:** Swedish

United's first signing of summer 2016 arrived from Swedish outfit Kalmar FF on a three-year deal to end weeks of speculation linking him with a move to the Championship.

Antonsson, who was the Swedish top-flight's leading goalscorer at the time of his switch to Elland Road, previously worked under assistant coach Pep Clotet during his time with homeland side Halmstads BK.

The striker enjoyed a prolific run of 22 goals from 40 matches prior to joining United, and Antonsson marked his first start for his new club with a brace in a pre-season friendly victory over Shamrock Rovers in Ireland.

SOULEYMANE DOUKARA

D.O.B.: 29/09/1991 | **NATIONALITY:** Senegalese

The French forward, who is eligible to play for Senegal due to his parents, moved to United from Italian side Catania in summer 2014, with his initial loan switch made permanent after just two months in England.

Doukara, a trialist with AC Milan as a youngster, enjoyed a rich vein of form in front of goal at the start of 2016, netting four times from six matches, including the quickest of the season – after just 12 seconds – in a 2-1 defeat away to Ipswich Town.

The striker was suspended for eight games towards the end of last term for biting Fulham's Fernando Amorebieta.

MEET THE BOSS

Garry Monk

Date of birth: 06/03/1979

Birthplace: Bedford, England

Playing career: Torquay United, Southampton, Stockport County, Oxford United, Sheffield Wednesday, Barnsley, Swansea City

Playing position: Central defender

Teams managed:
Swansea City, Leeds United

Twitter: @GarryMonk

"I haven't come here to do the average or be mediocre," was Garry Monk's rallying call following last June's appointment as the new man in charge of Leeds United. "The Premier League is what we are here for and we can't shy away from that."

His opening words were bold but Monk's ambition has been evident throughout a career which has spanned from playing in League Two to becoming a Premier League manager at the age of just 34 – the division's youngest at the time.

"I'm a young manager but I'm not a manager that wants to take the easy route," he claimed. "I want to have challenges put in front of me – and big challenges."

Monk embraced a number of sizeable challenges during his 11-and-a-half-year association with Swansea City, with the South Wales outfit playing in League Two but plotting a rise through the divisions at the time of the defender's arrival from Barnsley back in 2004. Fast forward seven remarkable years, and Swansea's 2010/11 campaign culminated in Monk skippering the side to Premier League promotion via a Play-Off final victory at Wembley.

Two-and-a-half top-flight seasons later, and still the club captain, Monk was tasked with stepping in as player-manager and halting Swansea's perilous slide towards the relegation zone following the departure of Michael Laudrup.

Safety was secured with two games to spare and Monk's impact in the hot-seat prompted Swansea to offer the centre-back the job on a permanent basis, handing him a three-year deal. The Swans' faith in Monk was rewarded the following season as he led the club to a highest-ever Premier League finish of eighth with a record points tally of 56.

It was an achievement which led to links to the England job and another new contract at the Liberty Stadium. Expectations were high heading into

2015/16 but Swansea struggled to recreate the fine form of the previous campaign as results slipped, and Monk was relieved of his duties shortly before Christmas.

A brief spell out of the game followed, with Monk spending his time visiting a number of clubs across Europe, including Europa League champions Sevilla, to gain new ideas and insight in preparation for his next challenge. That would come six months on from his Swansea exit as a new era began at Elland Road.

"We all know the history of the club and the standing it has in English football," said Monk in his opening press conference. "The passion of the fans, the history and the ambition of the owner all ties in with what I wanted to do. I want to be challenged and really get my teeth into a big project. That was the underlying factor throughout the whole process and that's the reason why I'm here today."

BACKROOM STAFF

Pep Clotet
Assistant coach

James Beattie
First-team coach

Darryl Flahavan
Goalkeeping coach

GETTING TO KNOW YOU

We spoke to members of the Leeds United squad to find out what makes the players tick and uncover some interesting facts about their life on and off the pitch...

Lewie Coyle

Tell us about your remarkable sporting family...

"There are four brothers – Tommy is the eldest, he's a professional boxer and he's achieved a lot already. Then there's Joe who's trying to make his way in the professional golfing game, there's myself here at Leeds and then our youngest brother, Rocco, he's torn between football and boxing. He's playing at Hull City's Academy and boxing at Tommy's gym."

Chris Wood

Were you good at any sports other than football when you were growing up?

"I played a bit of cricket and rugby and was okay at them both. But I'd grown up loving football and I really enjoyed it. When I first moved to England, the football here did take some getting used to as it's so much bigger than in New Zealand."

Pablo Hernandez

Who was your footballing idol when you were growing up?

"Michael Laudrup when he was playing for Barcelona and Real Madrid. I always bought shirts – from Barcelona to Ajax – with his name on the back. I'm a lucky man because I was able to play for him for a year with Getafe in Spain and nearly two years at Swansea."

Kemar Roofe

What would you be if you weren't a footballer?

"Probably something in business, whether that's with property, cars or doing my clothing line with my brother."

Alex Mowatt

Who is the cleverest player in the squad?

"I don't think there are too many, to be honest! But I'll say Woodsy because he sounds quite posh!"

Hadi Sacko

Who is your best mate in the Leeds United squad?

"I grew up in the same building as Toumani Diagouraga in the suburbs of Paris. I was on the second floor and he was on the fourth floor until Toums left to go to Watford. He used to come back quite often so we saw each other quite a lot even when he was playing in England."

Marcus Antonsson

Tell us something interesting about your birthplace...

"Where I come from in Sweden, it's out in the forest a little bit and maybe one or two thousand people live there. But a lot of them are Leeds fans! It's a place called Unnaryd, it's located in the forest a little bit – a little village. A lot of people out there are happy that I came to Leeds!"

Rob Green

What song did you choose for your 'initiation' when you first joined the club?

"Girls and Boys by Blur, which, amazingly, I soon realised that no one knew because they're a lot younger than me! When I say I sung it, I shouted it – one verse, one chorus and I was out! I was glad to get my song out of the way."

UNITED IN IRELAND

Preparations for the 2016/17 campaign truly kicked-off with a two-week stay in Ireland, where United played their first pre-season friendlies of the summer and enjoyed a vital period of team bonding with Garry Monk's summer signings.

TRAINING

The squad spent a fortnight training at the FAI's impressive Abbotstown HQ on the outskirts of Dublin, often spending their days working on double sessions and utilising the nearby gym and pool facilities. The two weeks spent together provided the perfect opportunity for Garry Monk and his coaching team to start implementing their new ideas, both physically and tactically, as they began to look towards August's season-opener away to Queens Park Rangers.

Assistant boss Pep Clotet explained: "All of the training sessions were designed to keep the players progressing and to take them forward. It was always based on the idea that we have for Leeds and the direction we want to go in. The facilities were fantastic and the set-up was unbelievable. It was a very good place to work because it was calm and we could focus. We also had fantastic resources at the hotel."

TEAM BONDING

Pre-season tours are traditionally prime time for team bonding exercises and United's summer trip to Ireland was no different, with the players and staff spending a day clay pigeon shooting at Courtlough Shooting Grounds in Balbriggan.

Once small-sided teams had been created, the group headed off to test their aim against a range of moving targets throughout the day, providing the new signings with the perfect opportunity to integrate with their new teammates away from the training pitch.

"I always find it important that we do some activities outside of the football," said Garry Monk. "It's something I'm very big on. It was a chance for the lads to have a bit of competition – you see a different side to their character and it's a good way to get them bonding outside of that football environment."

MEETING A LEGEND

One of the highlights of the pre-season tour came on the final day of training – when United and Ireland legend Johnny Giles paid the players and staff a special visit. Giles, who won two First Division titles, the FA Cup and League Cup among other silverware during his 12 years as a player at Elland Road, stopped by to chat to Garry Monk and his squad, before posing for photos with the team.

"It's great to come down and meet everyone", said Giles. "Leeds United was my club – I had great times during my 12 years there and it's nice to see them over in Dublin. I've got a few friends who are involved around this particular training centre and it's always nice to see the lads. I was just surprised they remembered me – they wouldn't have seen me playing as it was a long time ago! But they all seem like nice lads and Garry's a lovely chap – I had a nice chat with him and wished him all the best for the season."

MATCHES

Two friendly fixtures were played during United's time in Ireland and both ended in victory for Garry Monk's side.

First up were second division side Shelbourne, who welcomed around 2,500 supporters to Tolka Park to witness United's pre-season campaign get underway with a 2-1 win. Early goals from Souleymane Doukara and Hadi Sacko gave the visitors a comfortable lead, but Shelbourne pulled one back shortly after half-time to make it more of a contest.

United then travelled to Tallaght Stadium to face Irish top-flight outfit Shamrock Rovers and recorded another victory in convincing fashion – this time with Marcus Antonsson netting a brace either side of a Chris Wood penalty in a 3-0 rout.

2016/17 KIT LAUNCH

Our 2016/17 home kit was unveiled at an exclusive Elland Road event for Season Ticket Holders back in the summer, with Chris Wood, Kemar Roofe, Marcus Antonsson, Rob Green and Stuart Dallas all on hand to model Kappa's new design. The players were also joined by a selection of lucky Junior Season Ticket Holders, who proudly displayed the Greenpeace logo on their shirt, after an opening Q&A session with Garry Monk and his coaching team. Our club photographer was there to capture the action...

THE BIG
LEEDS UNITED QUIZ

Put your Leeds United knowledge to the test with our bumper quiz on all things white, yellow and blue...

1 Which player became the club's first signing of summer 2016?

2 At which two of our fellow Yorkshire clubs did United head coach Garry Monk spend time during his playing days?

3 Who was our top goalscorer for the 2015/16 season?

4 In which forthcoming year will Leeds United celebrate the club's centenary (100-year anniversary)?

5 Can you name the two Leeds United Academy graduates who were part of England's Euro 2016 squad?

6 What nationality is Garry Monk's assistant, Pep Clotet?

7 How many different goalkeepers featured in the United first team during the 2015/16 season?

8 In which year did United last win the league title?

9 Can you name the global environmental organisation whose logo features on the front of all Leeds United junior replica shirts?

10 Who progressed through the youth system to make their full United debut first, Alex Mowatt or Charlie Taylor?

Answers on page 58–59 – no cheating!

16 Can you name our Under-23s team coach who started his playing career as a youngster at Thorp Arch?

17 Which outfield player made the most United appearances during the 2015/16 campaign?

11 Can you name the four young players who signed their first professional contracts with the club last summer?

18 At which Championship stadium did our first game of the current season take place?

19 The club's 'Kop Cat' mascot shares his first name with which former United captain?

12 Which team did United beat at Wembley to lift the 1972 FA Cup?

13 The North Stand/Kop at Elland Road is named in tribute to which legendary former United manager?

20 Can you name the twin brothers who joined the club from Doncaster Rovers in January 2016 and have played regularly for our Under-21s?

14 What would be the total if you added together the squad numbers of Chris Wood, Stuart Dallas and Toumani Diagouraga?

15 True or false? Goalkeeping coach Darryl Flahavan once had a loan spell at United during his playing days.

END OF SEASON AWARDS:
THE WINNERS

We take a look at those whose performances were rewarded with silverware at the end of the 2015/16 season...

PLAYER OF THE YEAR

CHARLIE TAYLOR

Full-back Charlie Taylor topped the official supporters' vote to claim the headline prize following a fine campaign. Taylor ended the season with 43 appearances to his name in all competitions, despite being sidelined for two months after coming down with glandular fever.

The Academy graduate's highlight came in a 2-1 victory away to MK Dons, winning the penalty for Chris Wood to open the scoring before firing home United's second goal of the afternoon and his first for the club.

"I just concentrate on my football," said Charlie. "But the awards at the end of the season are a massive bonus. You don't really think about them until they actually happen – then it's brilliant and you're absolutely buzzing about it."

YOUNG PLAYER OF THE YEAR

LEWIS COOK

For the second season running, midfielder Lewis Cook collected the club's Young Player of the Year award after another eye-catching campaign.

Cook, who was also named the Football League's Young Player of the Year, featured 47 times in all competitions during 2015/16 and scored his first senior goals along the way.

"It feels great to pick up awards at the end of the season and I was really proud to be named as the Young Player of the Year for a second year in a row," said Lewis. "It was a hard season for me but this was a good way to end it. I just need to keep on trying to improve and getting better."

PLAYER OF THE YEAR
AWARDS

LEWIS COOK vs FULHAM

Lewis Cook picked up his second trophy of last season's awards night for the stunning, long-range goal which secured a point at home to Fulham.

The England Under-19s international opened his Championship account in spectacular fashion at Elland Road, firing the ball beyond former United goalkeeper Andy Lonergan and into the top corner from around 35 yards out.

"Normally, I'd choose to pass it from there, but something just told me to shoot," Lewis explained. "I need to try it a bit more now, I think. I've been trying to shoot more and I've been practicing it in training, so I was really happy to see it fly into the top corner."

PLAYERS' PLAYER OF THE YEAR

STUART DALLAS

Northern Ireland international Stuart Dallas was voted by his teammates as the Players' Player of the Year following an impressive debut season at the club.

Dallas' 49 games in all competitions made him United's top appearance maker last term, having quickly established himself as a regular in the side after arriving from Brentford during the summer. The winger also netted five goals along the way, including a stand-out double that won the game away to Birmingham City.

"I think I made the right decision to come here," said Stuart. "It's a massive club with a massive fanbase. The fans have been brilliant with me – they support the team through thick and thin and walking out at Elland Road is just incredible."

BOBBY COLLINS UNSUNG HERO

MANDY WARD

Presented by the family of former club captain Bobby Collins, this special annual award was given to Mandy Ward of the Leeds United Ticket Office after over 31 years of continued service!

GOALS OF THE SEASON

We take a look at six of last season's finest net-busting strikes…

CHRIS WOOD
vs Derby County

DATE: Saturday August 29, 2015   **LOCATION:** iPro Stadium
FINAL SCORE: Derby County 1-2 Leeds United

The undoubted highlight of Chris Wood's debut campaign with the Whites came during the opening weeks of last season away to the division's hot promotion favourites. Having arrived from Leicester City only a couple of months earlier, the New Zealand international truly announced himself to the Leeds faithful at the iPro Stadium with a ferocious 88th-minute winner from the edge of the area, clipping the post on its way beyond former United goalkeeper Scott Carson.

"It's always nice scoring goals. But it doesn't bother me if it's 30 yards or a tap-in – a goal is a goal to me! I'll take them as they come."

"I was going to shoot but I thought I was a little bit further out… They gave me a bit more time and I just thought 'I'm going to hit it'."

ALEX MOWATT
vs Cardiff City

DATE: Tuesday November 3, 2015
LOCATION: Elland Road
FINAL SCORE: Leeds United 1-0 Cardiff City

Alex Mowatt's first goal of last season proved to be well worth the wait as his trademark long-range strike was enough for Leeds to taste victory over Cardiff City for the first time in 32 years. After being invited to stride forward, the midfielder's left-footed effort whistled into the top corner from 30 yards out, ending United's eight-month wait for three points at Elland Road and sealing a first win for then head coach Steve Evans.

ALEX MOWATT
vs Huddersfield Town

DATE: Saturday November 7, 2015
LOCATION: John Smith's Stadium
FINAL SCORE: Huddersfield Town 0-3 Leeds United

Mowatt stole the show again with another spectacular strike just four days on from his winner against Cardiff – this time in United's Yorkshire derby demolition of local rivals Huddersfield Town. Struck from a similar distance to his first of the season, the Thorp Arch graduate's unstoppable second-half thunderbolt swerved mid-air as it flew past goalkeeper Joe Murphy to wrap up a convincing victory at the John Smith's Stadium, earning Mowatt another Man of the Match award.

"I definitely preferred this one. It was a derby game and that settled it, really, the third goal. They were never coming back from 3-0 down. I was well happy with it."

LEWIS COOK
vs Fulham

DATE: Tuesday February 23, 2016
LOCATION: Elland Road
FINAL SCORE: Leeds United 1-1 Fulham

Lewis Cook's first league goal of his career – coming in his 66th Championship appearance for the club – was a worthy winner of the Goal of the Year award at the end of last season. The England Under-19s international levelled proceedings at Elland Road with a wicked, dipping strike from the best part of 35 yards out, leaving former United 'keeper Andy Lonergan helpless as he desperately flew across the Fulham goal line.

"Normally, I'd choose to pass it from there, but something just told me to shoot. I need to try it a bit more now. It flew into the top corner. I was really happy with it."

STUART DALLAS
vs Birmingham City

DATE: Tuesday April 12, 2016   **LOCATION:** St Andrew's
FINAL SCORE: Birmingham City 1-2 Leeds United

Stuart Dallas bagged an eye-catching brace in United's 2-1 victory away to Birmingham City towards the end of last season, but it was his second of the evening which became an instant Goal of the Year contender. After opening the scoring with a low strike in the first half, the Northern Ireland international doubled his tally for the night with a thunderous 20-yard volley shortly after the break, teeing himself before leaving the Blues 'keeper stranded.

"You've got to take your chances to go in behind and, fortunately, I was able to control it and hit it. Sometimes they go in, sometimes they don't."

SOL BAMBA
vs Wolverhampton Wanderers

DATE: Tuesday April 19, 2016   **LOCATION:** Elland Road
FINAL SCORE: Leeds United 2-1 Wolverhampton Wanderers

Captain Sol Bamba ended last season in fine goalscoring form, including a thumping effort against Wolves which prompted the defender to admit: "I'll be lucky if I ever score a better one!" Bamba cushioned a pass from Dallas on his chest on the edge of the area, adjusted his body expertly and unleashed a sensational half-volley into the top corner to set United on their way to an impressive three points at Elland Road.

"As a defender, it's rare you find yourself in a shooting position on the edge of the box, so it was a great feeling to see it fly in."

SPOT THE DIFFERENCE

Can you spot the eight differences in this photo of Garry Monk talking tactics with Luke Murphy?

Answers on page 58-59

MEET THE SCHOLARS

These 11 young players are hoping to be stars of the future at Elland Road after signing two-year scholarship contracts with the club at the start of the season…

Alex Wollerton (midfielder)

Alfie McCalmont (midfielder)

Bobby Kamwa (midfielder)

Callum Nicell (midfielder)

Jamie Shackleton (midfielder)

42

Liam Kitching
(defender)

Matthew Keogh
(defender)

Moise Kroma
(striker)

Moses Abioye
(striker)

Robbie Gotts
(defender)

Samuel Amissah
(striker)

WORDSEARCH

Can you spot the names of 10 current Leeds United players hidden within our wordsearch?

B	E	M	P	V	Z	M	G	N
E	F	Z	G	K	U	N	Y	O
R	O	N	J	R	I	W	S	S
A	O	Y	P	L	E	A	L	S
R	R	H	Y	H	C	E	F	N
D	Y	A	M	K	D	N	N	O
I	X	M	O	W	A	T	T	T
E	L	Y	O	C	H	J	R	N
C	O	O	P	E	R	H	F	A

Antonsson

Ayling

Berardi

Cooper

Coyle

Green

Mowatt

Murphy

Roofe

Sacko

Answers on page 58-59

45

CHRIS WOOD'S DREAM TEAM

United striker Chris Wood becomes the gaffer and selects his dream XI of players he's come up against in his career…

Goalkeeper: Thibaut Courtois

"I played against him the season before last for Chelsea. He's just quality. He's a great player already and he's going to be a top, top 'keeper in years to come."

Right Back: Thiago Silva

"I know he's a centre-back but you could imagine him playing anywhere across the defence quite comfortably. He's just rock solid and a real leader for club and country."

Centre Back: Fabio Cannavaro

"I came up against him at the World Cup and he was just unbelievable with the way he read the game and picked balls up. He was a very good defender."

Centre Back: John Terry

"He's just solid, a proper defender. For years he's been one of the best around and he's still right up there. You know you're in for a battle against him."

Left Back: Marcelo

"You can see the quality he's got. I played against him at the 2012 Olympics when he was in the same Brazil team as Neymar. A class act."

Midfield: Steven Gerrard

"I came on at Anfield for West Brom against him nearly six years ago. He's been a top quality player throughout his career and he's totally unique as a midfielder."

Formation: 4-3-3

Midfield: Andrea Pirlo

"Another one I played against at the World Cup. He's unbelievable, his feet are a joke and his vision for a pass is just pure quality. He's still got it."

Midfield: Cesc Fabregas

"He's pure quality and has been since he first came through at Arsenal - he's a real technician on the ball. He's absolutely superb and would get in most teams."

Right Wing: Willian

"It was between him and Oscar at Chelsea, but I'll go with Willian for the pace and quality he's got. He fits into my 4-3-3. He had a very good season last year, too."

Striker: Didier Drogba

"He was my idol when I was a kid and I was lucky to play against him. He was so strong and physical, but also a great goalscorer. He had everything you want."

Left Wing: Neymar

"I played against him at the Olympics and he was just 'on flames' – no-one could get close to him. He was talked about massively at the time as the next big thing."

Courtois

Silva

Cannavaro

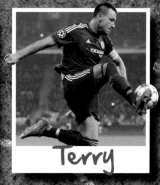

Terry

Marcelo

Gerrard

Pirlo

Fabregas

Willian

Drogba

Neymar

FIRST DIVISION TITLE WINNERS,
25 YEARS ON

Take a trip down memory
lane with photos from one of
the club's proudest days…

2017 marks the silver anniversary of Leeds United being crowned 'The Last Champions', as Howard Wilkinson's side famously pipped bitter rivals Manchester United to the 1991/92 First Division title in the final season before the Premier League was formed.

Wilkinson remains the last English manager to lift the top-flight trophy, and what made the achievement even more remarkable was the fact that it came just two years after United had secured promotion from the Second Division.

Leeds suffered defeat just four times all season and secured the title on the penultimate day of the campaign, beating Sheffield United in a 3-2 thriller at Bramall Lane before going on to lift the trophy the following weekend at Elland Road after beating Norwich City 1-0.

Leeds United 1991/92 First Division Title-Winning Squad:

Manager: Howard Wilkinson

Goalkeepers: Mervyn Day, John Lukic, Paul Pettinger, Neil Edwards

Defenders: Tony Dorigo, Chris Fairclough, Gary Kelly, John McClelland, Jon Newsome, Mel Sterland, David Wetherall, Chris Whyte, Mike Whitlow, Dylan Kerr, Ray Wallace, Rob Bowman

Midfielders: Gordon Strachan (captain), David Batty, Gary Speed, Gary McAllister, Chris Kamara, Steve Hodge, Glynn Snodin, Simon Grayson, Scott Sellars, Mark Tinkler, Andy Williams

Forwards: Lee Chapman, Bobby Davison, Rod Wallace, Eric Cantona, Noel Whelan, Carl Shutt, Imre Varadi, Tony Agana

LIAM COOPER

CROSSWORD

Can you answer the Leeds United questions below to complete the crossword?

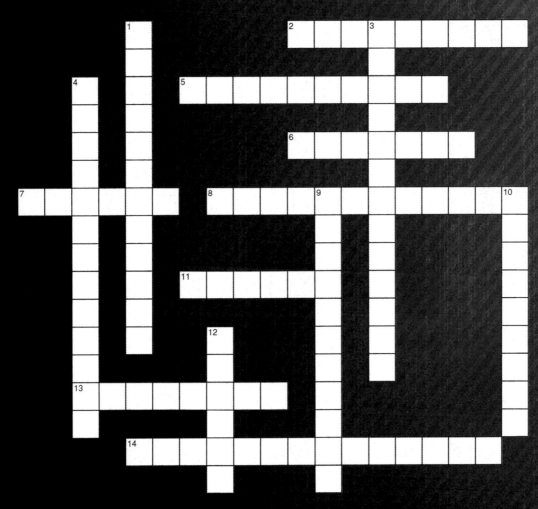

ACROSS

2 Who is Garry Monk's assistant at Elland Road? (3,6)

5 Chris Wood plays international football for which country? (3,7)

6 Where did United's summer 2016 pre-season tour take place? (7)

7 What was the League Cup renamed to at the start of the season? (3,3)

8 Which former England international is United's first-team coach? (5,7)

11 Our first summer signing of 2016 was born in which country? (6)

13 Which current first-team squad member has over 10 England caps to his name? (3,5)

14 Who was our second highest goalscorer last season? (5,9)

DOWN

1 From which club did Leeds sign forward Kemar Roofe? (6,6)

3 Who won the 2015/16 Player of the Year award? (7,6)

4 Can you name the young midfielder who made his senior debut on the final day of the 2015/16 season? (7,6)

9 Kyle Bartley and Matt Grimes joined on loan from which Premier League club in summer 2016? (7,4)

10 Which stand at Elland Road has two tiers? (4,5)

12 Which nationality is on-loan winger Hadi Sacko? (6)

Answers on page 58-59

51

ALL LEEDS AREN'T WE?
FAMOUS FANS

Celebrity Leeds fans who you may, or may not, recognise from the world of film, music and television…

Ralph Ineson

The Game of Thrones star is a lifelong United supporter and still attends as many games a season as his hectic acting schedule permits. Ralph has also featured in Harry Potter, The Office and Guardians of the Galaxy. He even had a brief role in the Damned United and his distinctive Yorkshire accent has seen him provide voiceovers for an array of television adverts.

Verne Troyer

Okay, the Hollywood actor and comedian has previously been pictured sporting an Arsenal shirt, but we'd like to think Verne is a convert to the way of the Whites after his recent visits to Elland Road. Verne, who is best known for his role as 'Mini Me' in the Austin Powers films, was in attendance for our 2-0 victory over Derby County in November 2014.

Chris Moyles

The radio presenter seizes any opportunity to reference United on his shows and has filled the airwaves with Marching on Together on several occasions, including the morning after his beloved club's famous victory over Manchester United in January 2010. Chris was born in Leeds and, although he doesn't get to Elland Road as often as he would like these days, he still follows our fortunes closely.

Other notable famous Leeds fans…

Josh Warrington (Boxer) • **Ed Miliband** (Politician) • **The Pigeon Detectives** (Band) • **Mel B** (Spice Girls)

Kaiser Chiefs

The Brit Award-winning Leeds band take their name from South African football team the Kaizer Chiefs – the former club of legendary ex-United captain Lucas Radebe. The Kaisers played a huge headline gig at Elland Road in 2008 and some of the band members can still be spotted cheering on United from the stands – home and away – providing they're not on tour.

Russell Crowe

The Gladiator star, a multi-award-winning actor, adopted Leeds as his team after watching Don Revie's great side on Match of the Day as a youngster. His brother chose Liverpool but Russell has stuck with United and was even linked with buying the club last season before ruling himself out, admitting he didn't want to spend any more time away from his children.

Kelly Jones

The Stereophonics frontman was born shortly after United won the league title in 1974 and has remained connected to the club ever since. A demanding touring calendar means Kelly is often jetting around the world, but he still keeps in touch with goings on at Elland Road. Kelly once presented good friend Wayne Rooney with a Leeds shirt with the Manchester United striker's name on the back.

Jeremy Paxman

The Leeds-born broadcaster, who hosted Newsnight on the BBC for 25 years, is a lifelong United fan and has an honorary doctorate degree from the University of Leeds. Jeremy lives in Oxfordshire now though, and is the current question master on University Challenge, meaning visits to Elland Road are difficult to squeeze in. He once interviewed fellow Leeds fan Ed Miliband in a live leadership debate.

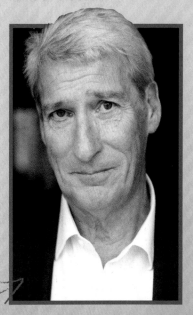

Other notable famous Leeds fans...

Chris Edwards (Kasabian Bassist) • **Jack P Shepherd** (Actor, Coronation Street) • **Colin Montgomerie** (Golfer)

MADE OF BRICKS

Elland Road, but as you've never seen it before…

In recent years, a number of intrepid football supporters have set about 'Doing the 92' – by paying a visit to every stadium in the Football League pyramid and ticking off a live match at each one on their travels.

This year, however, one nimble-fingered fan is embarking on his own unique 92-Ground Challenge… This one involves Lego bricks, and plenty of them!

As you can see from the pictures here, the early results are promising and we can hardly take our eyes off this 58x50x20cm model of Elland Road.

Creator Chris Smith told us: "I'm working on a project to build all 92 League grounds from Lego.

"There is no set order but I decided to build Elland Road to take it to the 'Yorkshire Brick Show', where it was then sold.

"It took about two weeks to build and contains over 1,500 bricks.

||||||||||||||||||||||||||||||||||||||||||||||||||||||||||||||||||

For more information on the pre-built Lego football stadiums, please visit **brickstand.co.uk** or email **brickstand@yahoo.co.uk**.

"I grew up in Bardsey, near Wetherby, so out of all the grounds, Elland Road is the one I've driven past the most and it was quite special to do.

"The stadiums are built by looking at lots of photos rather than going to the ground itself, as putting in too much detail wouldn't really work with the Lego.

"Out of all the grounds I have done, Elland Road was the most retweeted on Twitter, so I'd like to thank all the fans for that!"

A real work of art, we're sure you'll agree!

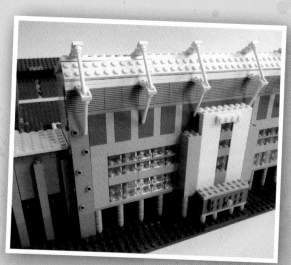

Follow

@LUFC
@ELLANDROAD
@LUFCTICKETS
@LUFCGRASSROOTS

LEEDS UNITED®

ANAGRAMS

Can you rearrange the anagrams below to work out the names of current Leeds United players?

 1 Compare Oil

 2 Doc How Sir

 **3** Boarding Tea Ear

 **4** Van Hip Kills Lip

 5 Unroll Bursts

 6 Fake Roomer

 7 Darts USA Tall

Answers on page 58-59

 8 Counts Masons Ran

QUIZ ANSWERS

Page 34-35 – The Big Leeds United Quiz

1. Which player became the club's first signing of summer 2016? **Answer: Marcus Antonsson**

2. At which two of our fellow Yorkshire clubs did United head coach Garry Monk spend time during his playing days? **Answer: Sheffield Wednesday and Barnsley**

3. Who was our top goalscorer for the 2015/16 season? **Answer: Chris Wood (13)**

4. In which forthcoming year will Leeds United celebrate the club's centenary (100-year anniversary)? **Answer: 2019**

5. Can you name the two Leeds United Academy graduates who were part of England's Euro 2016 squad? **Answer: Danny Rose and James Milner**

6. What nationality is Garry Monk's assistant, Pep Clotet? **Answer: Spanish**

7. How many different goalkeepers featured in the United first team during the 2015/16 season? **Answer: Three (Marco Silvestri, Ross Turnbull, Bailey Peacock-Farrell)**

8. In which year did United last win the league title? **Answer: 1992**

9. Can you name the global environmental organisation whose logo features on the front of all Leeds United junior replica shirts? **Answer: Greenpeace**

10. Who progressed through the youth system to make their full United debut first, Alex Mowatt or Charlie Taylor? **Answer: Charlie Taylor (2011)**

11. Can you name the four young players who signed their first professional contracts with the club last summer? **Answer: Ronaldo Vieira, Tom Pearce, Jack Vann and Michael Taylor**

12. Which team did United beat at Wembley to lift the 1972 FA Cup? **Answer: Arsenal**

13. The North Stand/Kop at Elland Road is named in tribute to which legendary former United manager? **Answer: Don Revie**

14. What would be the total if you added together the squad numbers of Chris Wood, Stuart Dallas and Toumani Diagouraga? **Answer: 28**

15. True or false? Goalkeeping coach Darryl Flahavan once had a loan spell at United during his playing days. **Answer: True (on loan from Crystal Palace in 2009)**

16. Can you name the coach of our Under-23s team who also started his playing career as a youngster at Thorp Arch? **Answer: Jason Blunt**

17. Which outfield player made the most United appearances during the 2015/16 campaign? **Answer: Stuart Dallas (49)**

18. At which Championship stadium did our first game of the current season take place? **Answer: Loftus Road**

19. The club's 'Kop Cat' mascot shares his first name with which former United captain? **Answer: Lucas Radebe**

20. Can you name the twin brothers who joined the club from Doncaster Rovers in January 2016 and have played regularly for our Under-21s? **Answer: Jack and Paul McKay**

Correct answers:

20/20: Congratulations – that's title-winning form! You're an expert on the world of Leeds United!

18-19: Well done – you're heading for promotion! There isn't much that you don't know about Leeds United!

15-17: Nice work – you've reached the play-offs! A couple of marks short of silverware, but an excellent achievement nonetheless!

10-14: Good effort – a top-half finish is something to be proud of! It's a bright start and your knowledge isn't far off the best!

5-9: Unlucky – a bottom-half finish is never the aim! Another read through the Annual is sure to see an improvement, though!

Below 5: Must try harder – you're in danger of relegation! It's time to dig deep and prove you have the knowledge!

Page 40 – Spot the Difference

1. Player's left sock has no 'LUFC' scripture

2. Manager's right leg has no badge

3. Player's armband is orange

4. Blue sock on substitutes' bench

5. Kappa logo missing from left leg of player's shorts

6. Half middle stripe on the adidas boot on substitutes' bench

7. Cone added in the bottom left

8. Player's right sock has yellow trim at the top

Page 45 – Wordsearch

B	E	M	P	V	Z	M	G	N
E	F	Z	G	K	U	N	Y	O
R	O	N	J	R	I	W	S	S
A	O	Y	P	L	E	A	L	S
R	R	H	Y	H	C	E	F	N
D	Y	A	M	K	D	N	N	O
I	X	M	O	W	A	T	T	T
E	L	Y	O	C	H	J	R	N
C	O	O	P	E	R	H	F	A

Page 57 – Anagram

1. Compare Oil = Liam Cooper

2. Doc How Sir = Chris Wood

3. Boarding Tea Ear = Gaetano Berardi

4. Van Hip Kills Lip = Kalvin Phillips

5. Unroll Bursts = Ross Turnbull

6. Fake Roomer = Kemar Roofe

7. Darts USA Tall = Stuart Dallas

8. Counts Masons Ran = Marcus Antonsson

Page 51 – Crossword

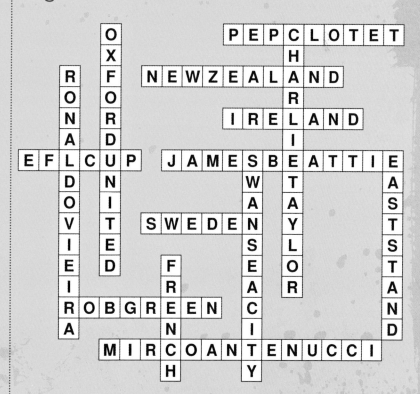

CLUB FACTS AND FIGURES

Elland Road capacity:
37,890

Elland Road pitch measurements:
115 x 74 yards

Nicknames:
'United' or 'The Whites'

MATCH SEQUENCES

Unbeaten start to the season:
29 (1973/74)

Most successive wins in all competitions to start season:
8 (2009/10)

Longest undefeated run:
34 (Oct 1968 – Aug 1969)

Longest undefeated run at home:
39 (May 1968 – March 1970)

Longest undefeated run away:
17 (Oct 1968 – Aug 1969)

Successive home wins (league):
15 (Jan 2009 – Oct 2010)

Successive defeats (league):
6 (April 1947 – May 1947)

Successive games without a win (league):
17 (January 1947 – August 1947)

Longest run without a home win:
10 (February 1982 – May 1982)

Longest run without an away win:
26 (March 1939 – August 1947)

First choice colours:
White with blue and gold trim

Change colours:
Yellow with blue strip

First game in Football League:
August 28 1920, Division Two v Port Vale (a)
Lost 0–2

Record attendance:
57,892 v Sunderland FA Cup 5th rnd replay
March 15 1967

Record League win:
8–0 v Leicester City, Division One, April 7 1934

Record European win:
10–0 v Lyn Oslo, European Cup 1st rnd 1st leg
September 17 1969

Record FA Cup win:
8–1 v Crystal Palace 3rd rnd January 1930

Record League Cup win:
5–1 v Mansfield Town 2nd rnd, September 1963

Record League defeat:
1–8 v Stoke City, Division One, August 27 1934

Record European defeat:
'0–4 v SK Lierse, UEFA Cup, 1st rnd, 1st leg, [day]
Sept 1971 / Barcelona, Champions League, [day]
Sept 2000

Record FA Cup defeat:
2–7 v Middlesbrough 3rd rnd, January 1946

Record League Cup defeat:
0–7 v West Ham 3rd rnd, November 1966 /
Arsenal 2nd rnd, September 1979

> Leeds United came into being late in 1919 but it was 1920 when the club gained election to the Football League.

Record League scorer in a season:
John Charles 43, Division Two 1953 – 54

Highest number of league goals in a match:
5, Gordon Hodgson v Leicester City, Division One, October 1 1938

Highest number of League goals in aggregate:
Peter Lorimer 168

Record all-time goalscorer:
Peter Lorimer 238

Record appearances in league matches:
Jack Charlton 629

Record all-time appearances:
773 Jack Charlton / Billy Bremner

Record transfer fee paid:
£18m to West Ham for Rio Ferdinand, November 2000

Record transfer fee received:
£29.1m from Manchester Utd for Rio Ferdinand, July 2002

Oldest Player:
Eddie Burbank (41yrs and 23 days) – v Hull City, April 1954

Youngest Player:
Peter Lorimer (15 years and 289 days) – v Southampton, September 1962

First schoolboy to play for club:
Tom Elliott v Norwich City, February 3, 2007

Most players used in a season:
44 (2004/05 and 2006/07)

MANAGERS

Dick Ray 1919 – 1920

Arthur Fairclough 1920 – 1927

Dick Ray 1927 – 35

Billy Hampson 1935 – 1947

Willis Edwards 1947 – 1948

Major Frank Buckley 1948 – 1953

Raich Carter 1953 – 1958

Bill Lambton 1958 – 1959

Jack Taylor 1959 – 1961

Don Revie 1961 – 1974

Brian Clough – 1974 (July-September)

Jimmy Armfield 1974 – 1978

Jock Stein 1978 (Aug – Sept)

Jimmy Adamson 1978 – 1980

Allan Clarke 1980 – 1982

Eddie Gray 1982 – 1985

Billy Bremner 1985 – 1988

Howard Wilkinson 1988 – 1996

George Graham 1996 – 1998

David O'Leary 1998 – 2002

Terry Venables 2002 – 2003

Peter Reid 2003 (Mar – Nov)

Eddie Gray 2003 – 2004

Kevin Blackwell 2004 – 2006

Dennis Wise 2006 – 2008

Gary McAllister 2008 (Jan – Dec)

Simon Grayson 2008 – 2012

Neil Warnock 2012 – 2013

Brian McDermott 2013 – 2014

David Hockaday 2014 (June – August)

Darko Milanič 2014 (September – October)

Neil Redfearn 2014 – 2015

Uwe Rosler 2015 (May – October)

Steve Evans 2015 – 2016

Garry Monk 2016 -

Can you spot our furry mascot within the crowd of Leeds United supporters at Elland Road?